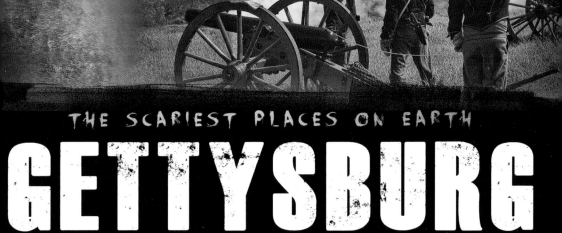

THE SCARIEST PLACES ON EARTH
GETTYSBURG

BY MICHAEL FERUT

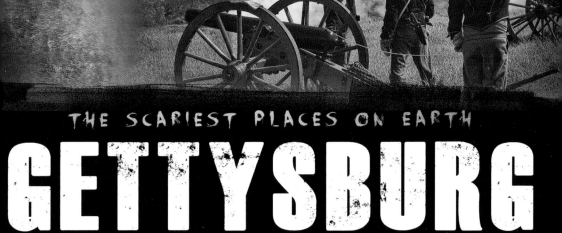

BELLWETHER MEDIA · MINNEAPOLIS, MN

Are you ready to take it to the extreme?
Torque books thrust you into the action-packed world
of sports, vehicles, mystery, and adventure. These
books may include dirt, smoke, fire, and chilling tales.
WARNING : read at your own risk.

Library of Congress Cataloging-in-Publication Data

Ferut, Michael, author.
  Gettysburg / by Michael Ferut.
     pages cm. -- (Torque. The Scariest Places on Earth)
  Summary: "Engaging images accompany information about Gettysburg. The combination of high-
interest subject matter and light text is intended for students in grades 3 through 7"-- Provided by
publisher.
  Audience: Ages 7-12.
  Audience: Grades 3 to 7.
  Includes bibliographical references and index.
  ISBN 978-1-60014-995-5 (hardcover : alk. paper)
  1. Haunted places--Pennsylvania--Gettysburg--Juvenile literature. 2. Ghosts--Pennsylvania--Gettysburg-
-Juvenile literature. 3. Gettysburg (Pa.)--Legends--Juvenile literature. I. Title. II. Series: Torque
(Minneapolis, Minn.) III. Series: Scariest places on earth.
  BF1472.U6F47 2014
  133.1'29748'42--dc23
                                        2013051344

This edition first published in 2015 by Bellwether Media, Inc.

Printed in the United States of America, North Mankato, MN.

TABLE OF CONTENTS

CHAPTER 1

UNKNOWN SOLDIERS

You are visiting the battlefields of Gettysburg, Pennsylvania. Your guide leaves once the tour ends, but you continue to look around. All of a sudden, gunshots ring out.

You look into the distance. Men in **Civil War** uniforms are marching toward one another. They fire their rifles and charge. It seems real, but you think they must be actors.

Later, you see the guide and ask about the battle you saw. The guide says that there were no **reenactments** today. Who did you see fighting?

CHAPTER 2

A SMALL BOROUGH AND A BIG BATTLE

Gettysburg is a borough in southern Pennsylvania. It is the site of the deadliest battle of the American Civil War. Around 160,000 men came to fight at Gettysburg. More than 50,000 of them were killed or wounded. Some people say that the ghosts of soldiers still march and fight there.

Pennsylvania

Gettysburg

In 1863, the **Confederate Army** was moving north. They stopped at Gettysburg to find supplies. Instead, they found a bloody battle.

After three days, the **Union Army** won the battle. The Confederates had to **retreat** south. This was a big victory for the Union. It gave them the **momentum** to win the war.

LONE CASUALTY

Only one townsperson was killed during the Battle of Gettysburg. Jennie Wade was making bread dough in her sister's house. A stray bullet went through her door and struck her in the heart. She died instantly. Some people think her spirit remains in the house.

12

After the battle, many bodies were left in the summer sun for days. They were eventually placed in **unmarked** graves. Some people think their ghosts haunt the Gettysburg **cemetery** and battlefields because they never had a proper burial.

IMPROPER BURIALS

Many Union soldiers were buried in Gettysburg. Bodies of most Confederate soldiers were moved south. However, up to 1,500 missing Confederate soldiers might be buried in unmarked graves.

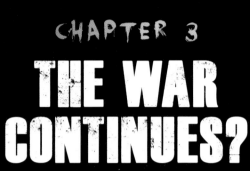

CHAPTER 3

THE WAR CONTINUES?

The battle left an eerie mark on the town. People see strange things where the fighting took place. Around town, people claim to see the ghosts of soldiers. Nearby, there is a bridge where soldiers were executed. Visitors say they can still feel their presence on the bridge.

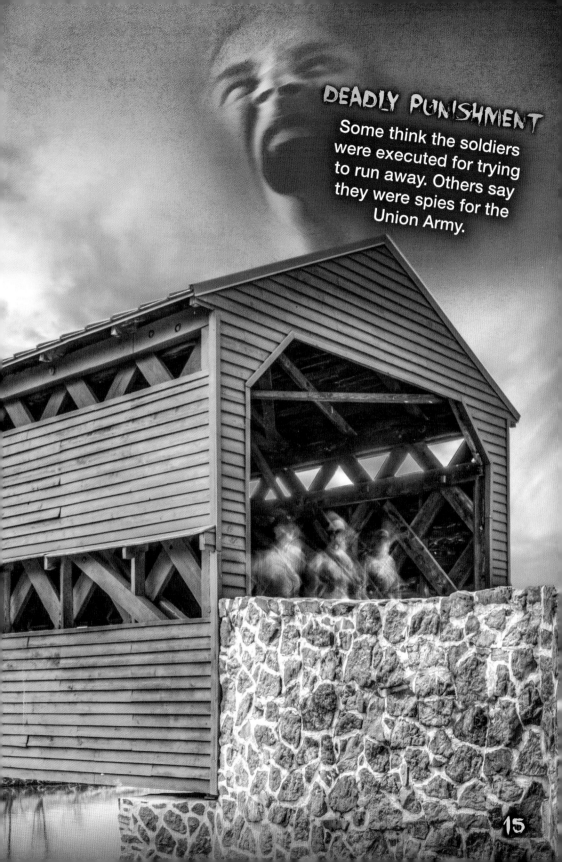

DEADLY PUNISHMENT

Some think the soldiers were executed for trying to run away. Others say they were spies for the Union Army.

15

Pennsylvania Hall

Many of the buildings of Gettysburg College were used in the battle. Pennsylvania Hall was a hospital for wounded soldiers. Now it is the setting of ghost stories.

Over 100 years after the battle, two college workers were using the elevator late at night. It stopped at the wrong floor. The door opened to a bloody Civil War hospital. Surgeons were busily operating on soldiers. The workers closed the elevator doors as quickly as they could. Neither could explain what they had seen.

Today, around three million **tourists** visit Gettysburg each year. Not all visitors see ghosts, but many have strange experiences. Some cameras stop working on the battlefields. Others still work, but the photos show ghostly figures that the visitors did not see at the time.

PARANORMAL PICTURES

Visitors have said that ghosts even helped them take photos. At the Devil's Den, some say a ghost showed them the best spot to take a picture. Their descriptions of the ghost match the appearance of soldiers that might have died there.

To this day, more U.S. soldiers were killed at Gettysburg than in any other battle in history. There are many terrible stories about the difficulties soldiers faced. Are the ghosts of these soldiers still fighting on the battlefields?

GLOSSARY

borough—a community that is smaller than a city or is a smaller part of a city

cemetery—a place where the dead are buried

Civil War—the war between the northern and the southern states; the American Civil War lasted from 1861 to 1865.

Confederate Army—the army that fought for the southern states in the Civil War

eerie—strange and scary

executed—to be put to death for breaking a law

momentum—a strength or force that is very difficult to stop

reenactments—performances of an event that happened in the past

retreat—to be forced back from a battle because the enemy is winning

tourists—people who travel to visit another place

Union Army—the army that fought for the northern states in the Civil War

unmarked—when something has no words or signs telling what it is

TO LEARN MORE

AT THE LIBRARY

O'Connor, Jim. *What Was the Battle of Gettysburg?* New York, N.Y.: Grosset & Dunlap, 2013.

Rajczak, Michael. *Haunted! Gettysburg.* New York, N.Y.: Gareth Stevens Publishing, 2013.

Stanchak, John. *Civil War.* New York, N.Y.: DK Pub. Co., 2011.

ON THE WEB

Learning more about Gettysburg is as easy as 1, 2, 3.

1. Go to www.factsurfer.com.

2. Enter "Gettysburg" into the search box.

3. Click the "Surf" button and you will see a list of related web sites.

With factsurfer.com, finding more information is just a click away.

INDEX

The images in this book are reproduced through the courtesy of: justasc, front cover (top), pp. 6-7, 20 (ghost right); Pgiam, front cover (bottom); Croisy, front cover (skull); Nagel Photography, pp. 2-3 (background), 4-5; Juan Martinez, pp. 8, 9; (Collection)/ Prints and Photographs Division/ Library of Congress, pp. 10, 16-17; William H. Tipton/ Wikipedia, p. 11; Maxime VIGE, pp. 12-13; Mkopka, pp. 14-15; Coast-to-Coast, pp. 18-19; Tetra Images/ SuperStock, pp. 20-21 (background); Evan McCaffrey, p. 20 (ghost left).